Race to the Rich in Recession

Race to the Rich in Recession

Table Of Contents

Foreword

Chapter 1:
Introduction

Chapter 2:
Recession Races

Chapter 3:
Recession Gold Rush

Chapter 4:
Getting rich in a Recession Gold Rush

Chapter 5:
The Tricks in the Recession Races

Chapter 6:
How to Always be the Killer Winner in A Recession

Chapter 7:
How to Make Triple Your Money in Recession

Chapter 8:
The Secrets and Tips for Recession Race

Wrapping Up:
The Best Strategies and Legal Implications in Recession Race

Foreword

Economic recession seems to be a reality in life. It is also an aspect of ebb and economy flow. You may notice that there are some instances that the economy is in great development. Likewise, the economy faces some changes at times while there are also some instances that the economy recedes and declines. If ever you notice that this particular situation happens, you should not panic as there is no reason for you to panic and be frightened, most especially if you are prepared for it.

Recession Race for Riches
How to Take Advantage of a Recession Gold Rush to Get Rich

Chapter 1:
Introduction

Synopsis

How does economic recession affect an average individual like you?

The Basics

Maybe you have this question in your mind right now. To make it clearer for you, this book will tell you everything you need to know about recession races. From this book, you will gain an in-depth knowledge about this economic situation, which will help you a lot in winning the race for riches during a recession.

This book is full of interesting facts and ideas about recessions. The book discusses the ways to deal with this crisis.

This book is intended for everyone and for the businesses and companies as well. The main aim of it is to help the readers in coping up with economic recession and winning the race.

Economic recession might be a scary matter and it is full of challenges for an average person and companies or businesses located in any part of the world. However, everything will be fine and winning the race through the recession period is possible if you know what to do. It is the right time for you to learn more about this.

Enjoy reading!

Chapter 2:
Recession Races

Synopsis

When the economy is in a recession, expect that there would be a race for all persons who want to become rich even if the economic condition is not good. This aim is possible for everyone and if you are aiming for this, you have to believe that there is a great chance for you to do so. You can do it if you know what you need to do so that you will win in the race. Recession races happen around the world today and there are people who get rich and win in these races.

The Race

Becoming rich during a recession appears to be an oxymoron. You have to keep in mind that credit is rigid when there is a recession. There are fewer jobs to offer and if people will try to become rich during this situation, they will strive for it against each other. This is how the race will start.

If you want to join the race and become the winner, there are certain things that you can do to get more chances to make the economic recession a great opportunity for you to prosper. There is no need to change the usual way you live. Instead, you have to rise up and be brave to face the impact of the challenging economy.

If you see that it is applicable, you can try to become more productive in your present job. You may ask for overtime to raise additional income. Make the management of the company where you work impressed with your work ethic and be keen on details. Second, you have to assess your budget and refrain from spending your money on unimportant things so that you can save money. Always remember that spending less and being wise in buying are helpful to anyone who wishes to prosper even while the economy declines.

Also, you may opt to change your driving habits. You can sell your low gasoline mileage car and replace it with a more efficient one or you can even choose a public vehicle. Always maintain the car to improve its efficiency and to lessen your repair expenses. If you are planning to go back to school, you may look for financial assistance options available. These offerings will let you pay the expenditure after you graduate.

You may also sell all your unwanted items in your garage. Offer a garage sale or you may use the auction websites or online classified ads to liquidate the excess and to pay your debt at the same time.

During an economic recession, people tend to look for the items they need at cheaper costs.

Also, you should monitor the bond and stock markets from time to time. Markets usually fluctuate more throughout a recession. To win the race, you need to be updated with the statistics for unemployment rates.

Financial races happen every time a recession affects the economy of a country. There is nothing wrong if you aim for riches even if the economy's condition is not good. To win, you have to do the steps mentioned above. With your strong determination to achieve success, winning in the recession race will not be hard for you to attain.

Chapter 3:

Recession Gold Rush

Synopsis

If the global economy is under the influence of full-fledged recession, what usually happens together with the economic turbulence is the modern-day gold rush. As the experts were able to say yes and express their acceptance of the fact, most of them stressed the advantage of gold investment throughout the times when the economy is under depression or recession.

The reason they want to emphasize gold investment is that it will keep them updated with the actual prices of gold in the market. The commodity has had inverse correlations together with the world's economy.

Primarily, if the economy is in a down situation, gold will strive and will attempt to reach and create a record of high prices. All cash is backed up by gold and thus this commodity will be the safest investment in the market.

Gold Rush

On the other hand, as the opposite relationship between the world economy and gold is a powerful and a historically precise trend, nothing is a hundred percent sure particularly with investing. The best thing to do is to start investing your money in gold and in the other metals. However, you have to make sure that you have a consistent connection to the coin brokers, dealers and other firms concerned with gold investment. This way, you will get an idea about the actual price of gold.

Although gold is substantially more stable compared to any other commodity where you can invest your money, you should never stay too calm and believe that everything is fine. Always find out the recent price and the value of this commodity to ensure that all your investments are secured and safe. This will also enable you to track all your earnings to know where your money goes. Gold investment is not an investment that is typically included in the advertisements, but this is also a sound investment that you could make.

Purchasing gold when the economy is under recession is already a traditional strategy. During the year 1930, 1970s and 1980s when depression affected the economy, people went altogether to buy gold or silver and treated them as a safe haven. People who buy gold usually extend themselves too much for investing to stave off the decline of the economy.

Although the situations are not severe in the same way as the present scenario, the basic rule remains similar. People tend to abandon their investments for other commodities and they choose gold so that they can keep their funds. This will let them make money to get the amount they have invested. In the present economic landscape, this metal is among the investments that could help their financial health.

Chapter 4:

Getting rich in a recession gold rush

Synopsis

You know that gold is often among the best options when it comes to investment. The first among the gold rushes in the world revealed the fact that there are more people who are really eager to become rich. These people are those who are too much interested in this shiny and precious metal.

Way back before, gold was considered as one of those things that serve as the basis of the wealth of a person. Nowadays, this metal is accessible to all investors whether they are rich or average. It is obvious as even the countries with a smaller population are the major investors for gold. The main reason behind this is that this metal may go up higher in the succeeding years. Compared to any other investments, gold has a good value which can't be overlooked.

Getting Rich

Gold has been one of the most appreciated assets for several decades. Though investing in real estate used to be considered the best option, the present economic crisis and recession which conquered the whole world showed that it is not the best choice for investors at all.

Most of the investors who prefer to invest in real estate properties lose their money as it influenced the success of most creditors and most especially, those banks that are known to be the most firm ones around the world.

The question that you might have right now is "how do investors get more money if they invest in gold?" Becoming rich in a recession gold rush will be possible if you do the following:

> 1. Find out the actual cost of gold in the market today. Always keep in your mind that it will increase every day. If you will compare the cost of it with its previous costs before, you will see that it is higher than before. Some investors speculate that people expect a market bubble to happen. Therefore, you have to hurry up and buy gold while you still have the chance to do so. In some years, the cost of this metal will go higher and this will provide more chance for all investors to earn money and become rich.

> 2. Gold is always in demand and things may change around you. It is the result of innovations and advancements in technology. It is not the case when it comes to this precious metal. This has

been there for several years and it is always appreciated by millions of people around the world.

3. Those who want to invest in gold are the people who are really determined to become rich. Among the best means to prove this claim is by considering the way that the richest men and women of the world got all their money. These people invested their money in gold once and most of them preferred to keep on investing their money in gold.

These are just some of the reasons why most people became rich as they invested their money in this precious metal. So perhaps, gold is indispensable in most industries. This might be the right time for you to make an investment and choose gold. What you need to do is to begin purchasing small coins or bars of gold.

Chapter 5:
The Tricks in the Recession Races

Synopsis

Recession always results in a race and winning on it will lead to a better life. To survive and beat all hurdles to achieve success, you know that there are certain things that you need to do to attain your goal. However, taking precautionary measures and knowing what you should never do when there is a recession is also important. The following are the five things you should never do so that you can win the race:

Tricks

- Cosigning a loan – doing this is just like putting yourself deeper in the hole of economic deficit. In the event that the borrower of the money fails to pay his or her debt, you will be the one to pay that. When the economic condition is not good, the risks related to loan cosigning can be even more because it might become a reason for you to lose your job so both you and the borrower will not be able to make payments at all.

- Obtaining an adjustable rate mortgage – when buying a home, there are some people who choose the adjustable-rate mortgage or ARM. In some instances, this action might be advantageous. As the amount of interest is low, the amount to be paid per month would be low at the same time. On the other hand, what if you lose your job and the interest rate of the mortgage went higher while the recession begins? While the rate increases, the charged amount you need to pay every month might also go up.

In this situation, you may find that it is really difficult to look for money so that you can pay your obligation. Always bear in your mind that overdue payments and non-payment could have a huge impact on your own credit rating. This could prevent you from getting loans in the succeeding months.

- Taking on additional debt – asking for a new loan might not be an issue when you are capable enough to make payments for it. You can apply for it as long as you have a stable source of profit. On the other hand, what will happen if your source of living is affected by recession? What might happen to you if you lose your job? In most cases, unemployed individuals take the job opportunities with lower salary rates than their previous jobs just to sustain all their needs and to have money which they can use to pay their obligations. Unluckily, the amount to be earned is completely too far from the amount they earn from their previous jobs. When it happens to you, all your savings will be lost. So, if you are planning to get another loan today, think about it first and consider the possible consequences that may happen in case you lost your job. Taking new debts when there is an economic recession is full of risk and you have to be careful about this.

- Being careless in your job – during a recession, you have to realize that the companies, particularly the larger ones might be under the influence of financial pressure. When it happens, most companies will try to lessen their expenditures as much as possible. In other cases, they may result to scaling back to the operations of the company, like holiday parties. Sometimes, companies prefer to cut the bonuses they pay and the worse is that they are forced to terminate other employees so that the company can survive without having too many expenses. This is one of the strategies of the companies today as they know that having more employees will bring more expenses for them. As the employment status throughout the recession might be extremely sensitive, employees like you should do everything that you can to ensure that your employer will consider you as among the most valuable employees of his or her company. You can do this by coming to work early, spending more hours working and performing all responsibilities properly. As there is no guarantee that it could save you, it will be the qualities that your employer will appreciate from you.

- Taking risks while making investments – the owners of business are always thinking about their business and its future. They tend to look for ways to make their business grow. On the other hand, recession might not be the right time to invest. A good example of this is taking a loan to provide an additional space for products. What if your business fails to develop? Would you have money to pay the loan on time? When it comes to investment, you should be careful and you need to consider the probable consequences that you may experience when this situation happens.

Chapter 6:
How to Always be the Killer Winner in Recession

Synopsis

Recession is a race and everyone is aiming to be the winner. To make sure that you will be able to achieve your objective, you need to make sure that you are the "killer winner" in the race. Here are 7 tips that you can follow to be sure to win the recession race:

How To Be The Winner

1. Concentrate on opportunities and make contributions.

2. Look for the most effective means to make yourself be more productive in your job. Try to do more things in less span of time. Whenever you go to work, always make sure that you will be able to finish everything that you need to do for that day.

3. Make your own self be more valuable and you can do it by learning more through education. It might be the right time for you to enroll in an MBA program or study in a law school. These are good options for you, especially if this is your dream. Financial assistance programs for education are always available and you can apply for these whenever you need to.

4. Stay positive and ignore those people who think negatively. Always believe that your own destiny is different and there is something good that waits for you in the future. The influence of the people around you matters but they are actually not necessary.

5. Develop the core of your strengths. When you find that it is hard to look for a good job within the marketing management industry, you may proceed to other related fields such as salesperson most especially if you are good in this.

6. Always keep in mind that some people will grow and achieve success while others will remain in the same way they were before. During a recession, you will see some people who are savvy and hard working and they can do more compared to others as they believe that they can do everything to save their jobs.

7. Everything happens for a reason and the economy is not an exemption to this rule. Sooner, recessions will happen but this will not be permanent. All you need to do is to make sure that you are prepared to face this economic situation.

During the times when recession conquers the economy, people tend to concentrate more on retreating and cutting losses. Instead of this, you should focus on dealing with it, beating and making sure that you will win.

Chapter 7:
How to make Triple Your Money in Recession

Synopsis

Economic recession might be a scary situation but there are ways to face and overcome it. The first thing that you can do to fight recession is to do everything that can to earn more income. The main thing here is to take advantage of this situation and do everything you can instead of allowing yourself to be the victim. In fact, there are ways to make more cash even when the economy's condition is not good. Here are the steps you need to follow to make it possible:

Triple It

☐ Odd jobs and look for online and home-based jobs. These are among the best means to earn additional income. Everything you do where you can get additional income would help you a lot in overcoming recession. Inside the economy where all people are looking for the ways to save money, it will be better if you will use your skill to make goods or offer services that can help other people. When it comes to recession, offering peculiar job opportunities to your friends, neighbors or family could be a great way to make and earn extra income. Expenditures are inevitable even when the economy is under recession. When you have spare time after work, you may look for the freelance jobs available on the web. These opportunities will let you make more money, which could be more than your regular salary.

☐ There is a fact that some people are forced to sell their personal items because of the lack of stable source of money. This is the outcome when people lose their jobs. There are several people who are willing to vend their personal things like gadgets at cheaper prices for the sake of their urgent need for money that is triggered by recession. If you have some spare cash and you want something to buy, this could be the right time for you to do so especially if you know that somebody is selling the item you want. However, buying items which you do not really need yet would not be helpful if you feel the effect of recession. You should bear in your mind that you need to make more money and spend less of it.

☐   In recession, working extended hours might not be the best choice for everyone. For those people who are willing to do it, they will be able to make some additional money that they can add to their savings in the long run. When you are recently employed and you get nothing for your overtime, then it is not the option for you. It would be better if you will look for the career opportunities that will let you make and earn income. Making an effective financial plan is among the strategies to make more money even when there is an economic recession. Just be sure that you are aware of the ways that will really generate income so that you can focus more on attaining your goal.

Chapter 8:

The Secrets and Tips for Recession Race

Synopsis

Economic recession might be a usual aspect of the economy but it doesn't mean that dealing with this can be done easily. There are more people who suffer from this in some countries around the world.

As there are more problems associated with the industry of real estate economy and there are more people who lose their jobs, people start to worry about the possible things that may happen in their lives. When you have a good and stable job, recession will not be a big problem in your case but it doesn't mean that you just have to relax and do nothing about it.

When there is an economic recession, people might be affected in different ways. The way you will survive from this will depend on the way you deal with it. Here are the things that you can do to make sure that you will be a winner in the recession race:

Secret Tips

1. Be aware about recession and the possibility of when it may affect the economy of the country where you live. Listen to the news and be watchful of all events related to economy. By knowing the details about recession, you will be able to make a plan on how you will deal with this.

2. Save money. To lessen the impact of economic recession in your life, you should start saving money and spending your money in a wiser way. If you are not sure with your present job, take advantage of it. Work more as long as you can and keep the extra money you get for every payday.

3. Avoid wasting your money. When you buy something, make sure that you will use it to avoid wasting your money. Always keep in your mind that money is significant most especially during the times when recession affects the economy.

4. Make your loved ones understand recession and ask them to help you. Dealing with the recession in the economy and ensuring that you and your loved ones will be able to survive is a responsibility of each member of your family. Your son and daughter could also help you by ensuring that they avoid wasting the food served on the table and that they are wise in using water and electricity. These will help you a lot in reducing the monthly expenditures of your family for the utility bills and

food consumption. When the light is not in use, ask them to turn it off whenever they have to leave. Always remind your kids to turn off the television if they are not interested in the show at all. By doing these simple things, you will be able to save some money.

5. Ask your neighbors and encourage them to help you. When the economy is under the influence of recession, it means that all people who live in the affected country will suffer from the effects of this. Teach your neighbors about the things you know that will help in overcoming the negative impacts of recession.

Wrapping Up

The best strategies and legal implications in recession race

Aside from the average people who lose their jobs whenever the economy is under the influence of economic recession, companies and businesses experience even more of the negative effects. The negative condition of the economy can affect these organizations in several ways that include slower demand, crashes within the stock market and increasing unemployment rates. These are all the usual effects of recession in the companies regardless of the industries they belong to.

The following are the strategies used by the companies throughout the period when the economy of a country is under recession:

Retention

The main priority of all types of businesses during the recession period is to retain their employees if possible and its culture as well as the values so that they can keep all their existing clients. Most of the companies and businesses around the world tend to provide their employees with a lower amount of compensation and even some offerings like free meals to lessen the higher cost of expenditures of the company for a while. This strategy will last until the companies and businesses know that economic recession still affects the countries where they are located.

On the other hand, there are some economists who believe that the turnover will oblige the companies to spend more than 100,000 dollars for every mid-level worker they have. This will be done if certain factors such as interviewing, recruiting, training, lost production and hiring are calculated. When it comes to the values of business, marketing and its image, it is necessary to keep the true identity of the business during the period of recession whenever it is possible. Aside from its help in keeping the high credibility and morale of the companies, this would also show the customers the strength of the company and that it is still capable of answering the needs of its customers despite the negative effects of the economy.

Pricing

Most of the businesses tend to drop quickly throughout the recession. It is necessary to maintain the costs of the products or services they
offer on their neutral level while the short term cuts as well as the hasty deals of the business eventually cause a large rate of profit loss.

The economists see that the substantial cost appears as a panic

sign
that the consumers would recognize. They will attempt to abuse the company and change suppliers and this will cause the business or company involved to lose more in terms of its share. To prevent this situation, the economists argue that businesses should be

confident
and be aware of how far they will be able to compromise. When the companies work with new clients, they should recognize the opportunities and try to become accommodating to the clients as possible.

The economists also suggest that the items with expensive values should keep their prices to protect their image and credibility as high quality products that cannot be provided at cheaper costs. Those consumers who really want these products will continue to buy them even if the prices remain the same.

To accommodate the clients who are no longer capable of buying expensive products, the companies and businesses should form a product line that the economists call "flanking products". These are the products that could satisfy the needs of the average customers with lower product quality and that are offered with no free service delivery but with reasonable costs.

By providing these products to answer the needs of other customers, the companies and businesses will be able to accommodate more customers who cannot afford high cost products. Likewise, there are some customers who prefer to buy everything they need in their daily living with no trade-ins. Therefore, companies will be able to get higher sales without changing the usual costs of the products they offer.

If you are a business owner, you know that you need to take some actions to save your company and make it survive throughout the economic recession period. These legal strategies will be the ultimate measures that can help your business in surviving and winning the race that will lead to riches. These strategies are used by those companies which are in good standing in the industry despite of the negative condition of the economy.

www.ingramcontent.com/pod-product-compliance
Lightning Source LLC
LaVergne TN
LVHW020742090526
838202LV00057BA/6184